WOMAN BEFORE A GLASS

A TRIPTYCH IN FOUR PARTS

BY LANIE ROBERTSON

★

★

DRAMATISTS
PLAY SERVICE
INC.

WOMAN BEFORE A GLASS received its Broadway premiere at the Promenade Theatre, opening on March 10, 2005. It was produced by by Susan Quint Gallin, Mary Lu Roffe, Debra Black, Maria Cozzi, Morton Swinsky. It was directed by Casey Childs; the set design was by Thomas Lynch; the costume design was by Willa Kim; the lighting design was by Phil Monat; the original music and sound design were by David Van Tieghem; the production stage manager was Renee Lutz; and the assistant stage manager was Tammy Scozzafava. Peggy Guggenheim was played by Mercedes Ruehl. The understudy was Patricia Hodges.

CHARACTERS

PEGGY GUGGENHEIM is the sole character. She's in her sixties.

SETTING

Peggy Guggenheim's home in Venice, the Palazzo Venier dei Leoni on the Grand Canal. Early to late '60s. Part Four is in a gondola on the canal.

PART ONE: Morning, 1963. The garden.

PART TWO: Early afternoon, 1965. The bedroom.

PART THREE: Late afternoon, 1967. The library.

PART FOUR: Evening, 1968. On the Grand Canal.

WOMAN BEFORE A GLASS

PART ONE

It's a bright summer's morning in the garden. The stone throne is right of center stage. Light is bright sunlight and shades of green. Some large flowering plants are seen.

PEGGY. *(Off:)*

WHY? YOU'RE ASKING WHY?

(She enters barefoot, wearing a pair of extra large sunglasses and a long, white, elegant Fortuny gown with a large yellow stain across the back of the skirt. Her arms are full of dresses, several pairs of high heels, a large purse, a large bead necklace, a handful of earrings, and a sheaf of papers. Her lips are clamped on the stub of a smoldering cigarette. Shouting:)

'CAUSE I LOOK LIKE A VESTAL FUCKIN' VIRGIN IN IT, THAT'S WHY, AND THERE'S A YELLOW STAIN ACROSS THE ASS THAT LOOKS LIKE I LOST CONTROL OF MY BLADDER!

(Beat.)

Oh. *Buon giorno.* I did know you were out here. Also that … TV crew back there.
Well. They oughta be furious with me.
Who'd blame them? I was supposed to be out here ages ago.

(She waves to back. Shouting:)

CIAO, TELEVISIONE, SI! BUON GIORNO!

They're sweet! They're Italians.
SONO TARDE!
SONO MULTISSIMO TARDE!
I promised them, swore to them I'd be on time.
MI DISPIACE! MIA COLPA! MIA MASSIMA COLPA!
Only it ain't *mia colpa* at all!
I've been stabbed in the back by the only woman I've ever trusted.
A snake in the grass! A flowering Judas if you ask me!
Canaglia! Puttana! Squaldrina!

She's just lucky I didn't say any of that to her face!

Me with a houseload of guests, this TV crew back there,
an interviewer from RAI, AND *il presidente d'Italia*
due any minute and what does she do?
Says *"Vacanza,"* and walks out the door.
"Fuck vacanza," I begged her.
I was practically in tears.
To a servant, for God's sake!
"If you go on *vacanza* now I won't be able to take you back," I told her.
"Not this time. No, no!
I'll have to get someone else. I can't hire someone for a single day!
I'll have to let you go!" I said.

She only shrugged.
"Vacanza," she said.

"If you walk out now it's *finito!*" I told her. *"Capisci?"*

She didn't bat a Sicilian eyelash.
I could've strangled her.
Dragged her scrawny ass out front ... and thrown it in the Canalazzo.
Let her wash up on the gay boys' beach at the Lido.

(She laughs.)

That'd curl her Catholic hide!

I brought her out here first thing this morning.
Forced her to watch 'em set up all those cameras.

"Ecco," I said. *"La televisione,"* I said. *"Le cinepres,"* I said.
"Vacanza," she said. And went back down to her room in the cellar and started packing.
A cardboard suitcase, for God's sake!
I couldn't believe it.
Not even the Moroccan leather I bought her.

That and a … a *schemata.*
With grilled sardines in it:
heads, tails, entrails and all!
And a chunk of asiago.
To eat on the bus!

"Are you kidding me?" I asked her.
"I'll buy you a plane ticket. *Aereoplano!*
You'll be with your …
grandbabies in …
two hours instead of two days!
Just wait 'til tomorrow! That's all I ask!"

She didn't stop packing.
"How many grandbabies do you have to have before you stop running off to see the latest one that's dropped out?" I asked her.

She just crossed herself and went on packing.
I could have spit!

Every penny she gets goes to those grandbabies!
If you've seen one grandkid you've seen 'em all, far's I'm concerned.
They don't turn interesting 'til puberty.

And her closet's pathetic!
Two dresses! Black, of course.
An old mink I gave her.
Which she's never worn.
A pair of sandals, one shawl, and a thousand dollars worth of Moroccan leather suitcases that've never even been opened, I don't think.

Probably never will be unless she's planning to be buried in 'em.
Every penny I pay goes to those grandbabies.

"Pina! Pina Pona, please!
How often do I ask you for a special favor?"

"Ogni giorno," she said. *"Effery giorno, effery giorno."*

"Liar!" I screamed.
I couldn't help it. She was lying. I know she was.

I don't ask … every day,
and even so today's extraordinary!
Today's my most important day since coming to Italy!

"How many times," I asked her, "is *il presidente* … your *presidente,* going to come to my little palazzo to honor me? He's your *presidente,* not mine!"

She went like this.

(She forks two fingers over her mouth and spits.)

"E communiste!"
"Who cares?" I said. "He was elected!"

And she's from Sicily, for God's sake.
What's she think those guys are up to, tiddlywinks?

I said she could have two weeks off in June, but how the hell could I know *il presidente'd* be coming here?
In thirty *minuti,* for cryin' out loud!
And I haven't even fastened up my bra!
It could be JFK for all she cares.
It's GRANDBABIES *UBER ALLES!*

Vacanza my ass!
Can you believe the selfishness of the bitch?

(She looks to the TV crew and smiles.)

The blond back there in the baggy blue pants? That's the cameraman.

(She waves.)

CIAO, BLUE BOY, *CIAO!*
I saw him at the RAI studio.

DON'T COME TOO CLOSE, BLUE BOY.
PROFESSIONALLY, I MEAN.

Personally he can come as often and as close as he likes.

CIAO!

I'm always fascinated by men in baggy trousers.
The mystery of it all.
Who really needs them and who simply thinks he does!

I don't want him too close with that camera.
I'm a mess. A total mess!

I only threw this on so my tits wouldn't be flapping about …
and because it's a genuine Fortuny …
made by the man himself.
These very stitches made by his own hand!

Now I find champagne dried all across the ass!

(She dumps her armload of clothes onto the throne, digs out some diamond rings and puts them on, digs a pack of Gauloises out of her purse and lights one. She digs through the clothes.)

There's gotta be something here.

These are all the expensive ones.
I know 'cause Pina Pona arranges them by price, and these're from the expensive end of the closet.

I'm not rich you know. People think 'cause I'm Mrs. Guggenheim I'm rolling in dough.
But Daddy dropped out of the family robber baron business just before all the rest of his brood struck it rich! We were lowly millionaires, not billionaires like the rest of the crew! We were the poor relations.

So most of these are gifts! For years I allowed myself only one hundred dollars a year to spend on clothes so I could buy pictures … or send money to starving artists.
I found out it's not good for artists to starve. They die.

Most of these are from Mother. Mother, Mother, Mother … famous for saying that a beautiful gown goes a long way towards hiding an unappealing face.
She thought I should be a fashion plate.

Most of these are from her.
Except the one I'm wearing. I paid more for this gown than my first Picasso.

(She snubs out the cigarette, selects a dress and holds it up.)

This was on the floor.
My doggies have been sleeping on it, I think.
Or a raccoon!

(She tosses it on the ground and kicks it away. She selects another one.)

Orange? Orange?
Possibly.
Only I'd look like an orangutan, of course.
Of course I've looked worse.

(She sets it aside and selects another.)

This one's sweet!
Mother bought this. Isn't this sweet?
But tiny.
Oh, my God, it's Vionnet! A Madeleine Vionnet!
From Paris in the '20s.
It's older than God!
Older than most of you!
Forty if it's a day!
A museum piece! Are you kidding me?
Duchamp and I danced all night in this once.
Well I was in it. Not Duchamp.
Paris was a ghost town.

1940 and the Nazis were only 300 miles away.
They were confiscating and destroying all modern art.

And I had my children there, my collection.
For two months I'd been seriously, deliberately buying a work of art a day.
A painting or piece of sculpture. Something!
I'd made up a list of artists I wanted …
with Herb Read and Duchamp …
and I was buying as many on my list as I could.
Not just anything, mind. The best!

Why not? They needed money and I wanted art!

Then one night with the Nazis a stone's throw away
Marcel said we should go dancing
and we did.
I put on this dress
and we went to one of Paris' deserted chi-chi restaurants
and the orchestra played for us all night.
That morning I went right out and bought two of my Kandinskys.
I don't remember which.
In those days, believe it or not, I wore this.

(She tosses it on the ground and selects another.)

This one is …

(She checks the label.)

Chanel!
Oh no!
I look like hell in Chanel.
It always makes me look …
seriously rich.
I should give this away.

(She takes up a skirt smeared with several colors of paint.)

Oh. This I brushed against a fresh painting once.
I was mortified.

I offered to sleep with the artist if he'd like.
I only said it to be polite.
He said going to bed with me'd be like screwing W.C. Fields.
"Really?" I said, "How is it you'd know?"

He'd painted a mural for me, on canvas for my New York apartment, and it was glorious. Huge. Twenty-three feet by nine. Glorious, but a bit long, so I took a pair of scissors and cut eight or nine inches off one end and threw it away.
I mean, my God, are you kidding me, it was huge.
Nobody noticed.
Later, like a fool, I gave it to some college somewhere.
Now, of course, I could live a solid year off the eight or nine inches I threw away.
I've never cleaned this. Why should I?
Who else can wear a genuine Jackson Pollack?

Balenciaga!
Balenciaga was crazy for toreadors.
One of them stole this for me.
He was far more beautiful than this gown.
And the closest I've ever come to sleeping with bulls … despite rumors to the contrary.
Spaniards, you know.

He said Balenciaga never touched a single one of the toreadors. Just placed them about his house, like statues.
He too wanted to be surrounded by beauty, I suppose.

If it were cocktails or dancing or oral sex … this one'd be perfect.

(She tosses it on the ground and selects another.)

Dior. Torn.

(She tosses it on the ground and picks up a pair of jodhpurs.)

Jodhpurs?
What the hell are …
I wore these when John Holms and I'd go riding.

My lovely John Holms.
My hero of the Somme.
I haven't seen these …
I wore them the day of his accident.

I won't wear these.
Perhaps to meet God … if He ever shows up.
No one else.

(She sets them aside and selects another dress.)

This …
Oh, I know this one.
I keep it out of guilt.
Tanguy's wife gave me this. She didn't know I was sleeping with him at the time.

Oh, God!
Tanguy was the sweetest man I ever knew.
Like a boy, a winsome little boy in the body of a man.

You can see it in his landscapes, I think.
The innocence. The joy.
The other-worldliness of those lunar-like landscapes.

When he drank his hair stood on end!
No, it's true! Liquor affected him like that.
Straight up on end!
But only when he drank!
The more he drank the more his hair stood straight on end.

It was phenomenal.
And it was soft …
like the pelt of a very small, shy woodland creature.
I wanted to marry him.
I asked him to marry me.
And he said he would.
"But what about my wife?" he said.
"She'd be so lonely …
so very lonely!"

And …
of course …
he was right.
He was very … very right.

(She tosses it on the ground and selects another.)

This needs ironing!

(She tosses it on the ground and selects another.)

Schiaparelli!
Schiaparelli gave me this …
after I'd caught her in the arms of my date
at one of my very own parties.
I didn't care.
He was nothing to me …
but the next day this arrived
with dozens of baby roses,
I mean dozens and …
well, I never wore it.

My God! You realize there's a history of twentieth century designer gowns right here and I've nothing to wear! It's pathetic!

(She gathers up all the gowns, wads them up and stuffs them behind the stone bench throne.)

Here's a clue for you.
Any broad who's lived from the lace-up corset and marcelled hair all the way up to the up-lift bra ain't no spring chicken!

That's the problem.
Let's face it.
I ain't gonna live forever
and what'll I do with my children, my collection? I've gotta give it to somebody, and it ain't easy.

Mine's the most important private collection of twentieth-century Art in the world, and what am I gonna do with it?
I mean where'll it go?

What'll happen to it?
When I'm dead, I mean?

Every major museum in the world wants it.
Even my ugly uncle in New York wants it for his museum.
He ain't gettin' it! He's got this bitch of Baden-Baden, this …
Tyrolean TWAT working for him
who wrote me this …
letter,
this … insulting letter!

So he's out. He ain't gettin' it!
But everyone else is possible.

The Italians want it.
That's why *il presidente's* coming here. Are you kidding me?

The Italian government wants it.
They all do.

That's why the cameras are here,
why they're interviewing me.

They hope they're in the running.
And they are.
Everyone is … except my ugly uncle.

(She nods to TV crew.)

I told those TV people not to come close 'til I say so.

They can wait another hour for all I care.

You all can do whatever.
My palazzo's *suo palazzo!* Are you kidding me?
Fix yourself a drink if you want.
I did.
I'd just avoid the guest room, if I were you.

That pip-squeak Southern novelist
everyone's so crazy about's in there

with a couple of Russian soldiers he picked up last night
at Cipriani's an' those two look like they'd fuck a frog if it didn't jump.
So I'd steer clear of them if I were you.

Some things Dante didn't even think of!
Otherwise … feel free.
The place is yours.
See everything but touch nothing's the only rule!

Okay, I'm gonna have to deal with those guys back there.
Sooner or later.
The what-do-you-call-it interviewer
made up this list of questions …
le domande?

(She opens her purse and exchanges the sunglasses for a pair of reading glasses which are missing half the frames. She balances them on her face, then picks up the sheaf of papers.)

I made a list of my own 'cause …
most of theirs won't do.
Not at all.
Most of their …
domande
have to do with me personally,
my personal life.
When I had one
an' I'm not gonna talk about any of that on camera.
So I gotta straighten it out.

Per esempio, they ask … da da da, da da da …

(She reads some of them, moving her lips as she does so.)

"Suo padre" and ah … *"sua madre …"*
For example. My parents?
There's really nothing to say about them.
Mother's father …
well first of all BOTH my grandfathers
were peddlers.

Mother's father,
Granddad Seligman was born under a peddler's cart, for God's sake,
in middle Europe somewhere,
they all came from there, Jews of course,
went to America as a peddler and founded the biggest bank
in New York City.
So, really,
there's nothing there but
money, money, money.
So who cares?

Daddy's daddy
and Daddy and all six of Daddy's brothers
were copper robber barons,
so what's there to say about them?

Mother was a nobody.
I think she had sex exactly three times in life
because there were three of us,
so who can blame Daddy for a whole slew of mistresses,
plain or fancy?
Mother was dull as dishwater,
uptight,
negative
and a whiner.
Her siblings were all seriously mad.

And mother couldn't have been too whiffty herself 'cause she had this really annoying habit of repeating everything three times, three times, three times!

I loved her, of course, but still!

Daddy used to say she'd married him thrice 'cause at the altar she said, "I do, I do, I do!"

Once, when we were at Delmonico's
she ordered "a cup of cocoa, cup of cocoa, cup of cocoa,"
and the waiter brought her three.

She was furious,
but we loved it, and laughed aloud, which ladies weren't to do, of course,
so then she was furious with us.

And I never talk about Daddy.
He was a Guggenheim, of course.
That's why I'm called Mrs. Guggenheim,
because of him.

He was first and foremost a gentleman.
The only real gentleman in the whole slew.

He was beautiful and he died April 15th, 1912.
I still mourn the day, so …
End of discussion.
I was very young.
Thirt … thirteen.
He always said …
I was beautiful.

I won't talk about him.

(She looks at the papers.)

And here they ask about *mariti!*
Husbands!
How many have I had!
Well, see that's not clear.
Mine or other people's?
How many *gondolieri* are there, for God's sake?
Not to mention England, France, America and a couple of other continents thrown in.

I only made the mistake twice of marrying any of them myself.

I don't know if I just happened to get the two meanest sons-of-bitches in the bunch,
or whether men are naturally nicer to women
they screw casually on a social basis

than they are to their own wives.
But the less said about Laurence Vail and Max Ernst the better.

(Keeping on her glasses, she puts down the paper.)

Now.
I gotta do something about this bra.
All I need's *il presidente*
an' his entourage
comin' in here with my tits still hangin' out!

BELIEVE ME, BOYS! THIS IS A SPECTACLE YOU DON'T WANNA SEE.

(Here she can either put on the bra under the dress if the arm openings are large enough or she can do the following: Turn her back to us and drop the bodice to her waist and pull the bra across her back, so the bra cups face us from the center of her back as she fastens it in front.)

It's my kids they oughta be asking about.
Well … not Sindbad so much.
There are two of them.
And a mismatched pair if there ever was one.

They're both Vails, of course.
From Laurence, my first husband, Laurence Vail, the painter and novelist.

Sindbad's the oldest. He's … ah …
Well, 1923 so …
What is this? '63? He must be …
well he's forty, right?
I don't remember his birth date.
Sometime about now, I think.
Sindbad's made two mistakes with his life.
First he was born with my nose, the hideous Guggenheim nose,
and second, he's refused to do a damned thing about it.

(She has fastened the bra in front where she can see it with her glasses, then begins sliding it 180 degrees.)

At least I had sense enough to try to get mine fixed.
But not he!
It shoulda been done when he was a kid.
And it would have too
if I'd had custody of him,
but his father wouldn't hear of it!

Also he's done nothing with his life.
It's my daughter Pegeen we should be talking about.

(She now slips her arms, one then the other, into her bra straps.)

OKAY, GIRLS! IN YOU GO, ALLEY OOP!

(Now she turns towards us, bra in place, breasts covered, bodice still down. She tosses her arms up in triumph!)

VOILA!

(She curtsies very deeply.)

Grazie, grazie tutti!

(She puts her arms through the sleeves of the gown and pulls up the bodice.)

My daughter's the only one worth discussing.
First of all she's gorgeous!
A beautiful, natural Aryan nose, tilted-tip!
Blond!
Slim!
Gorgeous!
And she's an artist, you know.
An important one.
Someday the name Pegeen Vail will mean something.

It's harder for a woman to be recognized.
I'm trying to change that.
I've arranged for a museum in Finland to give her a show. It's costing a bundle, but hey! I'll print the programs and sell them myself for a kopeck apiece.

Or whatever Finnish money is. Dried mallard, probably.

She's the reason I've agreed to be honored by *il presidente,* anyway.
She needs SOME reason to be proud of me.
And the only reason he's doing it's my collection!
I'm too old … not to know that!
It's all anybody's really wanted from me for a long time.
That and a handout or two.

But you'll see when you're in the house.
Pegeen's work is extraordinary.
She had her very first exhibition in London in my very first gallery, the Guggenheim Jeune before the war.
You'll see.
My bathroom walls are covered with her work.
And they're delightful!
Bright, colorful pictures of little girls. Skinny! Wide-eyed and innocent!
Each standing naked and alone.
Looking scared!

Charming!

She was in art school everywhere.
Not that you'd know it.
She's a Primitive. She's retained the …
charm and innocence the …
simplicity her work had when she was a girl.
Someday her name will be up there with …
well, I don't know. The blessed few of her generation.
Something like that, I think.

(She picks up the sheaf of papers again.)

Now there's something here I gotta talk to the producer about.
Il productore?
NO CANI, CAPISCI?
NO PHOTOS OF *MIEI CANI, CAPISCI?*
NO, *NEIN, NIX!*

(During the following she leans against the stone throne and tries on sev-

eral pairs of high-heeled shoes. Some don't fit, some the wrong color, etc. As she rejects a pair she hurls them — one shoe at a time — off left.)

In Venice they call me *"la Americana con i cani,"*
but I don't want any pictures of my little doggies.
My Lhasa apsos.

I won't allow any press near them.
Call me crazy! But!
I remember the Lindbergh case thirty odd years ago.
We all know how that one turned out.
I live in terror my babies'll be kidnapped.
What could I do? I'd give up my entire collection for my babies.
In a trice! I'd have to!
So I don't let the press photograph 'em.
Four are locked away for the day, and five are at the hair salon!

(She thinks she's found the shoes. she tries them by walking around.)

Now they say they're gonna ask me about art! Modern art.
Well.
They can forget that one.
We don't have all day.
Art …
modern art, anyway,
is never an answer.
It's always a question.

You ask what it is and why I collect it.
I can't answer that.
Look around this garden.

(She points into the audience.)

That's a Brancusi!
Those are Max Ernst, my very own ex-Max, I call him!
There's a Henry Moore.
Over there Jacques Lipchitz,
Pevsner,
Arp,
Giacometti.

I don't know if you've ever heard their names or not.
But twenty-five years ago they were mostly unknown.
I discovered them,
I encouraged them,
I started sending them monthly stipends so they could live
or play or pay their rent or feed their kids
or drink or whatever else they wished
just like regular, ordinary human beings.
But they're not regular, ordinary human beings.
They're extraordinary. They're artists.
Marvelous artists, and nobody wanted their work.
Except *moi!*

Later, when we go inside you'll see my collection,
nearly 200 works by the gods an' goddesses of modern art.

You may not recognize the artists's names but
believe me it's true: Braque,
de Chirico, Rothko, Calder, Bacon,
Magritte, Tanguy,
Ernst, Miro, De Kooning,
Delvaux, and others.
Many, many others.
Jackson Pollack —
unheard of 'til I gave him enough money every month
to quit being a janitor and paint.
Eighteen Pollacks in this house.
And dozens of others I gave away,
so he'd be recognized as the harbinger of the century to come.
Which I knew, when I saw his work, he would be.
Which he was. Is, though he's dead now.
For art lives on.
And why modern art?

Well, I didn't like it initially.
I favored Renaissance art.
But when I was fucking Samuel Beckett in the '30s …
or when he was fucking me,
he told me if I didn't know what to do with my money
I should buy modern art.
"Why?" I said.

"Because it's living," he said.

And that stuck.

Him I wanted to marry,
but I was too much for him. I wore him out.
We didn't talk much.
Only drank champagne and fucked like rabbits.
But when he spoke I listened.

He took me to meet his pal James Joyce.
They'd sit not speaking for hours,
while Nora Joyce'd bore me to death
with domestic tidbits:
talking of their kids,
her cooking and recipes
and sewing.
And suddenly James Joyce would say four words
that absolutely made no sense whatsoever
and Beckett'd say something equally terse
and meaningless
and then they'd laugh like idiots over what, nobody ever knew.

Usually whenever Beckett saw me
he'd run from me on the streets of Paris.
Then show up in the middle of the night
with three or four bottles of champagne
and wouldn't let me out of bed for two days.
Not that I wanted him to.

But when he did …
I started looking at modern art.
Living art, he called it. So I started buying it.
Why not, I thought?
I could afford it.
It sure as hell wasn't for profit!
It was worth absolutely nothing.
I collected it because he convinced me it was a duty to preserve the art of our own time.
My own time.
A duty no one else was willing to do.

Save and preserve an art that was a response to the madness of a world in chaos.
A world where fascists were democratically elected in Italy and Germany and elsewhere.
A time when Adolph Hitler denounced modern art
as evil and decadent ...
and Jewish!

A time when Nazis were marching through the streets of Paris,
the City of Light,
and all the world was devoting itself to murder.

A time of madness and death and camps set up for the extermination of people like me.
And mine.
Peddlers and the daughters and wives of peddlers.
And the granddaughters of peddlers.

In Paris, in 1940,
I begged the Louvre to hide my collection
from the Nazis and they sent
a man to my apartment on the Ile St. Louis,
looked at my collection and said,
"Je suis désolé, madame,
mais je ne vois rien ici
qui vaux le peine."

Nothing here worth saving, he said.

And I smashed the frames
and rolled the canvases up in my suitcases
and stuffed the sculpture
in crates of pots and pans
marked "Household Goods"
and smuggled them to the south of France
and then to America
where I was still told to my face that modern art can only be loved ...
by Jews.

And I thought ...
Vaffanculo!

You hear!
Vaffanculo tutti quanti!
You're right! You're absolutely right!
We Jews understand it because wherever we are,
wherever we go
we're always forced to always be outsiders.
And because of that we see this art for what it is —
not an answer —
but a question.
It's why Hitler wanted to destroy it all.
Because it forces us to see and feel and think differently and anew.
And for ourselves.

There was a very old critic here
named Berenson …
who spent most of his life
studying the paintings in Venice.
The Bellinis,
Tintoretto,
Veronese, Titian,
and my favorite artist Giorgione.
I met the old man
and invited him here.
He said, "Oh no, Mrs. Guggenheim,
your pictures would upset my stomach."

I told him if he'd only come I'd turn every one of them to the wall.
He was a hero to me.
I'd read all he'd ever written 'cause Laurence Vail
said I wasn't intelligent enough
to understand Bernard Berenson, so I read them all.
Seven volumes.

And I learned from him what makes a painting great.
The line.
The quality of color.
The tactile value, et cetera.
The unity of tone, et cetera.
The painter's soul, his anima reflected in the paint, et cetera.
How the work of a particular painter relates to that of the other artists of his time, et cetera, et cetera.

So I was so excited when he agreed to come
I had all the pictures covered or turned to the wall,
and sent one of my gondoliers to bring him here.
And I went to the front of the house to watch for him on the Grand Canal.
And when I saw my gondola approaching
I was standing beside the huge equestrian statue
Marino Marini made for me called, "The Angel of the City."
It's a young, virile man on horseback
and greeting the world and life — with his arms flung out like this.
And his phallus, huge and erect,
filled with
joie d'vivre.
And when I saw Mr. Berenson approaching the house
I shouted, "Mr. Berenson! Here! Up here!"
and I waved and waved.
And suddenly
Guido, my gondolier, stopped rowing.
And then the gondola slowly turned 'round
and went away.
I couldn't believe it.
And Guido said
Berenson had ordered him to take him back.

He said, "Tell Mrs. Guggenheim,
unless she covers that huge phallus,
and hides it from public view,
I'll never come there again."

Perhaps that's the answer.
The real answer.
Perhaps it's just …
uncovering the phallus after all.

(She roots in the jewelry.)

I can't find the other earring.
The hell with it.
I've been known to wear mismatched earrings before, so —
what the hell.
I'll look like one of Marcel's paintings.

Mismatched earrings nervously descending the stairs.

(She scoops up the earrings and dumps them behind the stone throne. Then she sits on the throne and smiles.)

Okay.
Pina Pona can go to hell!
I'm ready!
Bring on *il presidente!*

The first time I met him he pinched me so hard I was black and blue for two weeks.
It was all I could do to keep from slapping him.
This time I'll keep my distance.
And if I don't turn my back
he'll never see the stain on my dress.

OKAY, BLUE BOY!
YOU CAN BRING THOSE CAMERAS IN NOW IF YOU WISH.
AND BLUE BOY … PROMISE ME:
WHEN THE TV CAMERAS ARE ROLLING,
PROMISE ME NONE OF YOU'LL SHOOT A CLOSE-UP OF MY ASS!

(She smiles. Lights dim.)

End of Part One

PART TWO

In the bedroom. At rise stage is empty. Up left is a door to the bathroom. Down right is a low dresser. Attached to it is a very large oval frame … without the mirror. When Peggy sits there she seems to be looking into a mirror but in fact she's looking at us. During this scene she'll move between the dresser and the door. Sometimes she'll sit at the dresser, sometimes stand at the door. Sometimes she'll pace between. On top of the dresser is a telephone with buttons. The sound of running water comes from bathroom.

PEGGY. *(Off:)*

PEGEEN! SWEETHEART? PEGEEN!
I'M FINISHED!
BATHROOM'S ALL YOURS!

(Sound of knocking on a door.)

HONEY?
YOU AWAKE?

(Sound of knocking on a door.)

TIME TO GET UP, HON.
I'M OPENING YOUR DOOR SO WE CAN TALK!
BATHROOM'S ALL YOURS, NOW,
AND I'M DRAWING YOU A BATH!

(Sound of water running continues. Peggy enters from the bathroom. She wears a peignoir. Her hair is wrapped in a large bath towel. She goes to dresser and sits.)

She's wiped out!
Not me!

I feel great!
Nothing's as good as a soak in a big marble tub full of hot, scalding water!

Unless it's a Tanqueray martini,
extra dry, with a twist.
Or drifting in a gondola
at sundown …
while a glistening gondolier works his pole over you!
Here natives spend the first two hours after lunch in bed.
Everybody does. Even me!
Not alone, however! If I'm lucky!

WHEN IN ROME, HON, OR VENICE, YOU GOTTA ATTUNE YOURSELF TO THE *PENATES.* THE SPIRITS OF THE PLACE!

I could do with some right now, come to think of it.

(She opens drawer and lifts out a glass and a bottle of gin. She pours herself a stiff drink and re-stoppers the bottle, sets it back in the drawer. she studies her face in the mirror.)

Now what the hell am I gonna do with you?
Wish I could just peel you off an' start anew.

What's the name of that movie, that British movie where …
HON! WHAT'S THE NAME OF THAT MOVIE HAD THAT BAD BRITISH ACTRESS, FUNNY, WITH THE BIG EYES!
British!
We met them at a party Henry Moore took us to after the war and Pegeen was thrilled to meet the woman's husband?
THAT FAT LITTLE FAIRY THAT'S SO GREAT, HON!
THE ONE YOU LIKED.

Henry Moore took us there and he turned out to be gay as pink ink!
The actor, not Henry Moore.

It's his wife's movie.

She plays this …

creature-woman — this …
cadaver, this monster-woman
pieced together from body parts by a mad scientist so she can mar …
Bride of Frankenstein!

THE BRIDE OF FRANKENSTEIN, HON! REMEMBER?

This … monster woman's gonna marry Frankenstein.
So this mad scientist pieces her together!
See that's what I mean!
Instead of being PICKED APART by men as women usually are …

This woman's pieced together.
By this scientist.

Men have always … picked me apart.
Lawrence liked my legs.
And ass.
Max my stomach.
Sam my tits,
left one more'n the right.
And John Holms … liked everything.

Even my nose.
We women aren't like that!
If we love a man, we love the whole man!
All my life men have picked me over like a baked chicken.
Nothing left but bones an' gristle.

(She downs the drink, wipes glass with a tissue and sets it back in drawer and closes the drawer.)

Tonight's gonna be great. I can't wait.

TONIGHT'S GONNA BE GREAT, SWEETHEART!
COME ON! ARE YOU KIDDING ME?
YOUR FIRST ONE-WOMAN SHOW IN VENICE?
IT'S FABULOUS!

I can't believe it's taken me this long to think of it.
HONEY, ARE YOU UP?

(She exits into bathroom.)

Thatta girl!
Up an' at 'em!
That's my sweetheart.
YOU'RE EXHAUSTED.
But it'll pass.

(She reenters and bends completely forward from the waist and rubs her head with the towel.)

I SAW IT THE MINUTE YOU GOT OFF THE PLANE LAST NIGHT.
I DON'T KNOW HOW YOU DO IT REALLY!
She plays slave-wife to what's-his-name Ralph!
MOTHERING ALL THOSE KIDS?
PAINTING?
IT'D KILL A HORSE.
OR AN AMAZON!
AND YOU AIN'T EITHER, HONEY.
YOU GOTTA TAKE BETTER CARE OF MAMA'S BABY GIRL.

Thank God she gave Jean custody of the two oldest!
She'd never be able to paint!

And now in spite of everything
she's starting a whole new family with what's-his-name-Ralph!
She won't listen to me!

I'LL NEVER UNDERSTAND THE OBSESSION MEN HAVE WITH THEIR OWN SEMEN, HONEY!
It's gotta be theirs or nobody's.
What difference does it make? A kid's a kid.
If any man ever once got pregnant they'd all scream "birth control" so loud even Pope John the Twenty-third'd snap to!

Pegeen and Sindbad were more'n I could handle.
An' I had that … Doris person they were both so crazy about.

Even after Laurence took Sindbad …
I still felt overwhelmed.

And that was just with Pegeen.
And she was an angel!

Sweet … talented …
and no trouble.
And quiet! Thank God.

One reason I gave Sindbad to his father …
was all the noise he used to make.
And I adored Sindbad.

REMEMBER HOW NOISY SINDBAD USED TO BE?
THAT'S WHY I GAVE HIM TO YOUR FATHER!
I thought it only fair Laurence have one of them.
I SURE AS HELL WASN'T GONNA GIVE UP YOU!
YOU'RE AN ARTIST!

Really. Go in there later — the bathroom — and see her paintings.
You'll see.

You could see it when she was a kid.
An artist!
The only thing Sindbad's ever drawn's
the monthly checks I send him.
This one was drawing from the time she was three!
Kid stuff, but hey!

On the beach, in the sand, on the walls of the chateau.
I still have some crayon drawings somewhere. Juvenilia, but still!

HONEY — ARE YOU WATCHING THE TUB?

(She exits into bathroom.)

It's okay. Only half-full. YOU'LL SEE!

(She enters again.)

IT'S GOOD AS A DRY MARTINI.
Or a BELLINI.

Which I'm still gonna have Roberto make for her even if
she is on the wagon!
One won't kill her,
even with all the medication she takes.

I called her doctor in Paris this morning while she was tryin' to paint.
He said nothing's wrong with her a week away from that brood of hers won't cure.
He thinks it's nerves.

What we used to call a *crise de nerfs.*
Very popular in the Twenties.
All my girl friends had them.

Laurence had them all the time.
Laurence Vail.

Not me.
Even when he used to dump jam in my hair and walk on my stomach
it never affected my nerves.
That used to infuriate him! Drove him crazy!

I still haven't a nerve in my body. She gets those from him.
After we married he'd have two or three fits a week! At least!
Let's see.

(She works figures on a tablet.)

Married six years.
Six times fifty-two weeks a year, twelve, carry the one, three hundred and twelve weeks …
Times two fits a week …
giving him the benefit of the doubt …
Oh the hell with that!
Why should I give him the benefit of anything?
He beat me up! Tried to break my nose!
It was at least three tantrums a week!
Three times … three hundred and …
Holy shit!

Nine hundred and thirty-six!
Nine hundred and thirty-six hissy fits at least!
AND.
If I had a nickel for every time he made fun of my nose I'd be one of the rich Guggenheims instead of the poor!

Laurence threw a fit in practically every restaurant we ever entered.
She doesn't remember.
Most of 'em before she was born.
Sindbad knows.

Laurence'd throw food …
bottles … dishes … wine … silver …
Everything! Across the room!
We were barred from …
half the restaurants on the Left Bank …
and two-thirds of 'em on the Right.

And he blamed me!
Always!
Said I was trying to screw somebody!
The waiter or …
maître d' or …
one of his friends or …
or a customer or somebody!

And I probably was!
Who'd blame me?
The fool!

I met Laurence when Mother and I were in Paris in '21.
I was twenty-three … and still a virgin!
I decided this time instead of Peggy "doing Europe"
I wanted Europe to "do Peggy!"
We were in the Plaza-Athenee.
I saw Laurence in the hotel bar.
He looked like an Adonis to me.
So blond …
so Aryan I thought I'd faint.
I sent him a drink.
He asked if he could take me to my room.

I said *"Mais oui."*
He said that was all the French I'd ever need.
In my room ...
I handed him my postcards from Pompey.

(She laughs.)

The year after Daddy died Mother took us to Pompeii.
We saw all the frescos there
depicting all the ways people make love.
Mother and Hazel, she was youngest ...

They thought they were looking at wrestlers.
Benita and I couldn't stop giggling.
We each bought a whole set of those postcards,
and Mother said,
"I didn't know you girls had
so many friends,
so many friends,
so many friends!"
We couldn't stop giggling.

(She laughs)

At the Plaza-Athenee I gave them to Laurence.
I told him,
"I want to do all of these."

We did.
It nearly killed him.
Not me!
I loved it.

(Peggy exits into the bathroom. Sound of water being turned off.)

It's ready, honey. I want you to have a nice long soak.

(She reenters.)

YOU'LL SEE.
IT'S HEAVEN!

NOT LIKE THAT TUB YOU AND WHAT'S-HIS-NAME-RALPH HAVE IN PARIS.
NOBODY COULD SOAK IN THAT THING.

So much enamel's off their tub in Paris I'd as soon wash my face in the bidet as that thing.

(She throws off the peignoir and goes behind a screen.)

AND LOOK THROUGH THOSE PERFUMES.
I NEVER REMEMBER WHICH ONE YOU WEAR,
SO I BOUGHT EVERYTHING.
ALL THE GOOD ONES ARE THERE.

I WANT YOU CALM, COOL, AND COLLECTED TONIGHT, HONEY.

IT'S A BIG NIGHT!
AND IT'S ALL ABOUT YOU, HONEY!

TONIGHT I'M GOING TO BE SO MONDRIAN NOBODY'LL EVEN NOTICE ME! ALL HORIZONTALS AND VERTICALS!

(She comes out with one, then another rather plain dress and holds them before her mirror. Then goes behind screen again.)

AND THESE ARE ALL FRIENDS!
EACH ONE'S SAID THEY'RE SO EAGER TO MEET YOU.
GET TO KNOW YOU!

THEY'RE ALL HOPING YOU'LL COME OUT OF THAT FAMOUS SHELL OF YOURS!

AND ME!
DON'T WORRY ABOUT YOUR LOUD-MOUTHED MOM!
I'M GONNA FADE TOTALLY INTO THE WALL!

(She comes out with the most outlandish, bright, bold gown and holds it up, obviously selecting it.)

YOU'RE THE STAR! YOU'LL SEE!

THEY'LL BARELY NOTICE I'M THERE!

TONIGHT PALAZZO VENIER DEI LEONI IS YOURS!
I TOLD ROBERTO WHATEVER YOU SAY GOES!
YOU CAN MAKE US DANCE NUDE IF YOU WANT.

I WOULD!

AND EVERYBODY'S COMING, I MEAN EVERYBODY.

(She sits, puts foot on dresser, and begins giving herself a pedicure.)

Her father's coming,
With the latest Mrs. Vail.
I begged him not to.
He just said something spectacularly vile and hung up.

MARCEL'S DRIVING IN WITH HIS SISTER.
Don't ask, don't ask.
A whole truckload of ancient Surrealists and Cubists are training in from Grenoble.

STRAVINSKY AN' MADAM'LL BE HERE, OF COURSE.
GYPSY ROSE LEE AND ANNA MAGNANI WITH SOME YOUNG HUNK NAMED SALVATORE.
An' that little pip-squeak fairy I'm so crazy about says he's renting a roomful of male escorts and ... bringing them all up by train from Rome.
I said, "My God, Truman, they're cheaper here! I'll price them for you!"
"No!" he screamed. "Roman gigolos are far more acrobatic!"
I guess he'd know!

(She begins painting her toenails red, but runs out of polish.)

I told him, I'm not putting up swings!
I don't care if he brings a roomful of monkeys!

AND KIRSTEN'S COMING OVER FROM LONDON.
AND BALANCHINE.
I hear with some beautiful squaw.

Chester and Auden and some stranded truck driver they picked up on the Autobahn.
AND MARK AND MRS. ROTHKO AND …
well … EVERYBODY.
AND BELIEVE YOU ME
THERE'LL BE HELL TO PAY IF THEY DON'T ALL SHOW,
SO I THINK IT'LL BE QUITE A CREW!

(She digs in a drawer, takes out several empty bottles of polish, shakes them, checks with her broken glasses, then throws them back into the drawer. She picks up the phone and presses a button.)

Roberto, where the hell is Pina Pona an' what's she doing?
Well, tell her to stop that an' get Guido to take her to *la farmacia* in the gondola.
Don't let her walk!
I need toe paint, and I don't have all day.

Nail polish!
Tell her red, red, red!

Also, Roberto!
And this is important!
Tell her to get the eighty-five cent bottle American.
Six hundred lira.
Not the seven hundred lira one she got before.
And I mean it. I won't have her wasting twenty-two cents
like she did the last time.
It's for my toes, for God's sake!

And tell her I mean it!
If she does that again, I'll send her back.
I mean it!

(She hangs up.)

HONEY?

(She goes to the open door.)

Oh my God! Look at you, honey!

You're gorgeous!
Gorgeous!

You look *magnifica!*

SPLEN-DEED!

Oh, honey! Oh honey. I'm so happy you're here.
I get so lonely for you!
I know you're disappointed what's-his-name
and the kids aren't here,
but they'll be here next week all week.
I just didn't want him here now.

It's just so nice having you all to myself.
It gives us both time to … you know,
mother and daughter each other.

Sindbad has his wife and his ex-wife and his mistress
and his ex-mistresses
and his kids and her kids and their kids and our kids.

He doesn't care to come here anymore.
Without you I've nobody. No, no, I mean it!
You're the only one still in my life.
No really.

(Peggy returns to the dressing table.)

It's true.
She doesn't believe me but …
it's true.

She met Raoul last night. My beautiful Raoul.
She thinks he's something.
He's not.
Oh I'm fond of him but God!
He's younger than she is, for crying out loud!
I mean he's great, but … really.

Raoul's nothing but sex.

Great sex!
All day, all night sex,
with all the energy and eagerness of youth!

He's like a little puppy dog: all tongue and tail.
Like a puppy dog who's just found a new home!

He says I'm sexier than … Ridiculous, I know! Are you kidding me? But he does say I'll go down in history … which you must admit is spectacularly sweet and touching.

I've only really been crazy about one man.
My old soldier boy.
Hero of the Somme. John Holms.

He and Daddy … were the only men I ever loved who didn't beat me up or hurt me in some … really … spectacular way.

(She smiles.)

He even loved my nose.
Last thing … each night …
he kissed my nose.

(She laughs.)

"Sexy nose," he said.
"Sexiest nose … in Christendom."
When he died, that was sorta it.
In the love department for me I mean.
RAOUL'S NOTHING, SWEETHEART.
REALLY.
JUST SEX.
Nothing but sex.
Love built on sand.
NOT THE ROCK OF AGES KINDA STUFF I HAVE WITH YOU, KID!

Sindbad doesn't even call since I told him I'm not leaving any of this stuff to him. Or Pegeen. It's a treasure trove of art. I can't just leave it to anybody!

The Pollacks alone are worth a fortune!
So where'll it go? It's got to go to SOMEWHERE.
The Louvre, maybe. The Metropolitan Museum of Art or The Tate.
Any major museum.
Except my ugly uncle's museum in New York.
The Guggenheim!
It's not a museum.
It's a parking garage, for crying out loud!
Are you kidding me?
All ramps!
Uncle Solomon wants my collection, too, of course!
But he's got that soi-disant baroness!
That twat from the Tyrolean hills!
The bitter bitch of Baden-Baden!
And that insulting letter she sent me.
I'm not forgetting about that!
Are you kidding me?

Kandinsky was an old man. He NEEDED money.
A great artist!
The Nazis were coming. Everbody knew that.
It was only a question of time.
So I wrote my uncle for him! Him!
I'd already bought I don't know how many canvases
just to help him out.
I couldn't afford any more.
And he LOVED Kandinsky.
But he was under the thumb of this Tyrolean Twat
and busy buying all these third-rate paintings.
So I wrote my uncle, not HER.
And this cum-twat-cunt-slut German bitch of Baden-Baden …
this …Tyrolean twit, this twat par excellent,
this sleep-in mistress slash secretary
who'd styled herself an Aryan Baroness,
as much a Baroness as I'm a Vestal virgin,
wrote me, saying my uncle was above commercialism!
One of the original Robber Barons, mind you!

And that I was sullying the name of Guggenheim …
by buying and selling art.

I told the twat it was my name too
and impossible to sully more than had already been done.

So now they can beg for it on bended knee, for all I care.
I'll toss it in the Canalazzo before giving it to them!
Family or no! The bitch! My God!

And Sindbad, who wouldn't know a Picasso from a Rudolf Bauer,
will just have to get over it, but hey!
Without Pegeen, I'm nobody.

Nothing.

She's like my sister Benita to me.
I wish you could have known Benita.
She was the eldest. Sweet, so sweet,
loving.
Gentle, soft.
She walked into a room and everything stopped.
No one spoke.
Tall. Willowy.
Glistening raven hair.
Large, deep, dark eyes that smiled as surely as her slightly too-large mouth.

She'd enter a room …
everyone caught a breath and stared.

She came to England in '25, right after Pegeen was born.
Again when she was two.
She only came to see Pegeen.
She'd already had four miscarriages, but said Pegeen was so blond, so beautiful she wanted to try again.

When she died if it hadn't been for Pegeen, and having to care for her, I'd have died too, when she did.
I wanted to. Pegeen saved my life.

Laurence. Laurence Vail …
said, "You've mourned Benita long enough, for Christ's sake. She's only a sister!"

That's when I knew what a son of a bitch Laurence Vail really was and I had to leave him.

(Pause.)

When the *Titanic* … sank …
and all those lives were lost …
another ship … the *Carpathia* … picked up survivors, but nobody knew who they were.
Who lived or died.

There were thousands and thousands of people waiting,
hoping, praying their fathers too would be on that ship.
Their husbands and mothers and children and sisters.
And when it came into New York harbor, there was …
a hush so strong
sometimes I hear it still.

All the Guggenheims were there,
Daddy's brothers,
old granddad Guggenheim sitting stiffly in his carriage.
We didn't go to him.

Thousands of people huddled in the cold.
No one moving,
afraid to move as if we'd tip a balance.
No one.
Except for the horses stomping.
Nothing moved.
All staring up the harbor.

And then a cry, "It's coming! It's coming! The *Carpathia's* coming!"
And people pointing when they saw it.
And then … silence.
Everyone staring at the ship.
And it docked. And we searched the faces looking down on us, as though they were gods.
And lists were handed out.
And cries of joy and screams.
And screams.
And people … crying.

They'd reserved a space in the boats for all first class.
He put on his tuxedo: white tie, diamond studs and cummerbund.

I remember him like that when he took Mother to the opera and the ballet. And her gowns were heaven, but Daddy …
Daddy looked like a Prince,
a strong, virile young Arabian prince.

His brothers said he was the handsomest Jew in the history of the world. "Only since Solomon," he'd say.
And they'd say, "How do you know, how do you know?"
And he'd laugh … laugh.

(The bathroom door slowly closes.)

He gave his seat to a woman from second class and stayed on board.

And when we finally knew …
Benita held me and wouldn't let go.

I had chills and burned with fever.
I screamed and gasped for breath.
For days and days I couldn't breathe or else I'd hold my breath, and she'd pinch me
or pull me …
and wouldn't let go.
She was the oldest and loved him too, but she knew I was the one who wouldn't live without him.

Mother was useless.
Benita even comforted Hazel. But she held me, so I wouldn't die.

When Pegeen was three …
we were living out of London and an envelope came, tissue-thin, addressed, "Private: To Mr. Laurence Vail." I opened it.
21 AUGUST 1927.
BREAK NEWS TO PEGGY. STOP.
BENITA'S BABY STILLBORN. STOP.
BENITA DEAD. STOP.
SIGNED … SIGNED …

(Peggy looks in the mirror at herself. She looks at the reflection of the door and notices it's closed.)

Pegeen?

(She turns to face bathroom.)

PEGEEN?

(She runs frantically to the bathroom door and tries the handle. It's locked. She knocks frantically at the door and tries to open the door.)

PEGEEN!

(The door opens and Peggy steps back.)

Oh, I'm sorry! Forgive me!
It … it's just when I saw the door,
the bathroom door closed and you didn't answer.
I'm sorry. Forgive me …
I'm … I'm so …
It just brought back all those times, those other times when you …
No, no, I'm sorry.
It's past.
I know that's all past, behind us, I … I …
You … it's just …
you're everything to me, honey.
Forgive your stupid old, ugly mother!
I'm sorry honey, it's just …
You're my everything.
Really!
Oh, my God, honey! I was so scared!

Do you know how proud I am of you?
You're a brilliant artist, darling! An important one!
NO! The fact that you don't know is proof you are one!
Real artists are shy and sensitive and bashful and insecure and secretive and quiet. Not arrogant bastards like Picasso!

Do you know Picasso didn't want me owning his work? I wasn't good enough!

In 1940 I climbed up to this crappy little studio,
a sweltering hot Parisian summer, and stood there.
He looked at me and said,
"Oh no, madam! Wrong floor! Ladies lingerie is two floors down!"
The bastard!

(Peggy opens a drawer, takes out a glass and a bottle and she pours a very stiff drink and downs it. She pours another and holds it:)

But his paintings, Pegeen … his paintings!

I can't tell you how thrilling and inspiring,
how it fills me with hope and clarity
to know that all that genius,
all that beauty and magnificence,
all that razzle and dazzle and beauty …
emanates still in our time …
from such a small,
egotistical
and overwhelmingly ugly
little shit!

(Lights dim.)

End of Part Two

PART THREE

Late afternoon in the library. Lights rise on Peggy. She wears a muumuu and is talking on the telephone. The phone has two extremely long cords, twenty or thirty feet each. One is attached to the base of the phone, the other to the receiver. These should be exaggeratedly longer than is needed. As she talks she occasionally snaps the cord in front of her as if it were a whip. Occasionally she will kick it, or gather some of it up with her hand and throw it. Center stage is a long rectangular desk. She may sit on it or in a chair behind it or lie down atop it, etc. Across the back wall are three or five very wide horizontal lines abstractly indicating an extremely wide venetian blind. These horizontal lines run across a space of light that changes as the light outside changes. There should be a spectrum of color dissected by these lines. This is a long window onto the Grand Canal. Occasionally a breeze may ruffle these lines or cause the light from the windows to flicker. It is an autumn afternoon. Peggy smokes a cigarette and occasionally fans the air as if to rid the room of the smoke.

PEGGY. *(Into phone:)*

Forty.
No, I said forty. Forty million.
Hello? HELLO?
No the line is cutting in and …
Sir James?
Oh. These lines are terrible.
Especially in Venice. Something we Venetians live with.

(To audience:)

You'll have to give me a moment. This is a terribly important call.

(Into phone:)

I said it's valued at forty million at last year's rates. I SAID, AT 1966 RATES.

(To audience:)

It's Swinson. Sir James Swinson! Curator of the Tate!
Young for a curator.
Good-looking!
Told me the most wonderful news! I can't wait to …

(Into phone:)

Oh no, not lire.
Dollars. U.S. of A greenbacks.
And that's just for my children, you know.
No, no, my collection. I call my sculpture and paintings my children.
Yes. Yes.

(To audience:)

Told me the most glorious news about the bitch of Baden-Baden!
The Tyrolean twat?
Who works for my ugly uncle?
She's dead! DEAD!
Isn't that fabulous!

(Into phone:)

No, that doesn't include the palazzo.
The forty million's just for my collection.
My palazzo's worth twenty more at least.
Give or take a million.

(To audience:)

Can you stand it? The bitch is dead!
I nearly peed my pants for joy when he told me.
Dead, dead, dead!
When you're dead, you're dead, that's my motto.
And she's dead!

(Into phone:)

"Il Palazzo Venier dei Leoni."
No, I say "PALAZZO VENIER DEI LEONI!"
I don't know.
Perhaps the Venier family bred lions in it for all I know.

(To audience:)

Of course when he told me I gasped and gazed mournfully off … only for appearance's sake.
But if they don't cremate the bitch I'll fly over and dance on her tomb!
I am sooo thrilled!

(Into phone:)

Well, you have to see it!

(To audience:)

I can't believe he's never been here?
I think he's afraid of … .

(Into phone:)

No it's not one of those huge Venetian palazzos.
It's sweet.
It's small.
I call it my walk-in palazzo, my bungalow.
Venetians say it's unfinished 'cause it's only one story. But perfect for me.
The roof makes a tremendous sundeck.

I sunbathe there every spring and summer.

(To audience:)

Naked!
Across the canal they fill the windows to watch.
I wave and throw kisses.
They see my body as a harbinger of spring.

Whenever I'm up there naked they know winter's past!

(Into phone:)

Oh, it's easy.
It's all white marble and right on the Grand Canal. You can't miss it.
Right across from San Marco.
The Accademia and I are neighbors.
Yes, right next door.
They come here to borrow sugar.

Why don't you come?
Bring what's-her-name along …
Helen … or Blanche.
Your wife.

(Into phone:)

Susan, Susan of course! I adored her!
You can stay here,
everybody does. Are you kidding me?
Mio palazzo, suo palazzo to the whole civilized world and great waves of the uncivilized, too.

(Peggy puts phone down, lights a cigarette and talks to audience:)

He's afraid to come near me without his wife …
Stella or whatever.
Not my fault.
I lent my collection to the Tate last year
and they had this perfectly wonderful opening.
Champagne.
Caviar.
The works.
I was three sheets to the wind on champagne.
I didn't really know who the hell he was.
He's too young, too good-looking for a curator!
Are you kidding me?
And he was wearing these baggy trousers.
Green velvet, and baggy, baggy, baggy!

So just as that terribly homely, horse-faced, inbred little
princess they have over there crossed to greet me,
the museum director let out this …
this … shriek!
And lo and behold my hands …
both my hands …
were deep inside those lovely green baggy trousers.
And I really didn't know how they got there!
But I mean really!
Green velvet?
Are you kidding me?
What'd he expect?

(She picks up phone. Into phone:)

No, no, I'm here, but I haven't heard a word you said.
The sound went off and I didn't hear a thing.
Well …
I was saying I'd LOVE for you and what's-her-name Stella to be my guests.
No! I think it's important you see my children here, in their setting.
I was just telling someone here I can't believe you've never …

Hello? Hello? *Porca dio!* It did go out this time!

(She pushes a button on base of phone. Into phone:)

Roberto.
The line's gone out again.
Will you place the call for me?
Swinson. Sir James Swinson.
The Tate Gallery.
London of course.
Grazie.

(She hangs up and takes a deep drag on her cigarette, then snuffs it out.)

Oh the hell with that.

(She picks up phone and pushes button.)

Roberto, don't place that call.
Let him do it.
He's got the number.

(She hangs up.)

Fuck him! Why should it be on my dime?

(To audience:)

Now I have to do something with this ashtray.
I use them out of habit and it's MOST *verboten!*
Mussolini may be gone but Pina Pona lives!
All I need is for her to find traces of this!

(Now she deals with the dirty ashtray. She takes an empty wastebasket from under the desk and she dumps the contents of the ashtray into it. She realizes this was a mistake.)

Oh, *merda.*

(She takes wastebasket to window, picks out the butts and tosses them one by one out the window. She returns to desk and starts to set wastebasket on floor, thinks better of it and looks around the room. She goes to edge of carpet, turns corner back and considers pouring ashes there. She thinks better of that and straightens rug as phone rings. She goes to desk and sets wastebasket on desk. She picks up receiver and pushes button.)

(Into phone:)

Yes? Oh, just a minute.
Hell with it!

(She takes up her purse from the desk, opens it and pours ashes into it, closes purse, sets wastebasket on floor, and picks up receiver. As she talks she picks up ashtray and studies it.)

(Into phone:)

Yes, Roberto, put him through.
Ciao, Sir James.

Well, I told you!
We tried and tried to get back to you
but couldn't get through. The lines at this end are impossible.

(Suddenly there's a pounding on a door stage right.)

Oh! Could you hold for just a moment.
I just have to get rid of somebody.
(Again someone pounds on the door.)
Thank you so much.

(She goes stage right toward closed door.)

No, Pina Pona, you may NOT come in! Did you think I'd go back on my word? I don't even miss it, honestly, and I feel great.
Now, dear, I really have to get back on the phone.
It's a terribly important call.
Yes, dear.
Later.

(She returns to desk again. Into phone:)

Sir James, forgive me.
I've recently quit smoking and my maid promised my daughter she'd keep an eye on me, so whenever she thinks she smells the least HINT of smoke
she comes rushing in.

(Peggy takes a spray can from her purse and sprays the air.)

No, I've not found it difficult to stop at all.

The first couple of days were hell ...
but now I'm used to it.

All I wanted to say to you at my age
it's only prudent for me to look around for a home for my collection.
I want to level with you.
The Tate's not the only museum I'm cock-teasing about giving them my children,
my collection.

I've also been talking to the Metropolitan Museum,
the National Gallery in London AND in Washington.
And the Louvre.
Even my Uncle Solomon's museum in New York's been interested.
But it's not as easy as it …

(The telephone buzzes.)

I'm sorry Sir James.

(The telephone buzzes.)

Would you hold for a moment?

(She presses a button.)

Yes, Roberto?
Well tell Miss Pegeen I'm on a very important call now myself and I'll call her back when I finish.
Well, tell her this call is important too
and I'll call her back!
Now, please don't buzz me again until I finish with this call.

(She presses a button. Into phone:)

I'm sorry, Sir James.
I just wanted to say I'm insisting the collection and my palazzo stay together.
Sir James … Sir James … They must!
One's art is a reflection of oneself.
It's my life I'm discussing handing over to you.
Art is very personal.
It reflects who you are, how you think, what you feel,
your being.
It's my life I'm discussing handing over to you, my entire life.
This is the heritage I'm talking about giving you, Sir James, or someone.
This destiny, this heritage, the entire heritage of my life.

What?
Yes, of course, I'll hold.

(She hangs up the phone.)

He doesn't understand. How could he understand.
How can anyone understand?

(To audience:)

In Marseille in 1942 I gathered about me nine or ten refugees.
We were all attempting to escape the Nazis by flying to America.
I was staying in a little hotel, all alone.
It was before I married Max Ernst.
That wasn't to happen until we'd safely made it to the States.
But while I was in Marseille,
trying to smuggle my collection away from the Nazis,
and trying to rescue as many refugees as I could afford,
somebody pounded on my door in the middle of the night.
I was exhausted you understand.
From standing in lines day after day trying to buy exit visas, passports and identification papers for Marcel Duchamp and his mistress and Max Ernst and his sweetheart, and tickets for my two children, and somebody's doctor and his child,
and my ex-husband and his latest slut and so forth and so on.
And I opened the door and there stood three of the blondest and most beautiful young men I think I've even seen.
And they were all Nazis.
They seemed stunned,
and I realized,
it being the middle of the night I was stark naked.

So I turned on the lights and wrapped a sheet about me
while they tore the room apart.

I was absolutely furious
and exhausted,
and they demanded my passport and my papers.
Then one asked me in the most perfect French I'd ever heard to tell him if I was a *"juive."*
I looked at him,
and I thought I've not heard so much hatred put into that word since being a child
and we were all forced to leave a hotel in Vermont

because my little sister Hazel
had innocently admitted to the hotel clerk
that we were Jews.

So I looked at these three Adonises
and with all the force and fury I felt
I said,
"JE SUIS AMERICAINE!"
They asked my forgiveness and left.

I went to the lobby, still wrapped in the sheet,
to complain to the manager,
who told me
I hadn't any reason to be upset:
that I had never been in any danger.

After all,
he said,
the Nazi soldiers were simply rounding up all Jews.

(The telephone buzzes. She picks up the phone.)

Yes?
Sir James,
all I wanted to say is what I'm trying to preserve here
is
not just a random group of pictures
that can be scattered to the ends of the earth,

but a cohesive whole which can only exist here in my palazzo:
something quite fragile,
ephemeral: a reflection of one woman's dedication to the art of her time.

(The telephone buzzes.)

I'm sorry Sir James. Would you mind holding for a moment?

(She presses a button.)

Roberto, I've asked you not to …

Who?
What the hell does he want? All right, put him through.

(She presses a button.)

I'm sorry, Sir James. It's an emergency call from Paris.
Yes, my daughter and her children live there, so …
if you'll hold again.
Thank you.

(Phone rings.)

Ralph, what the hell's going on?
Yes she did call here,
but I couldn't talk to her.
If you're calling about the check it should have …

What do you mean gone?
Where's she gone?
Well what does the note say?

What does that mean, she knows about us? Oh my God.
Who told her that? No! No!
No, my servants would never …
Yes, I did fire someone. A gondolier. He was lousy, he was a thief!
No he wouldn't have!
Ralph, the pills, her pills? Did you check to see if they …

All of them? Oh God!
Ralph! Ralph, listen to me, listen, you filthy slimebag! You vomitous toad!
If anything … anything happens to her, I promise you
you will never see any of those children again!

(She slams down the phone. She picks it up and presses a button.)

Come on, come on, come on!
Roberto! Did Miss Pegeen leave a number? All right, all right, if she calls here again, put her through immediately, do you understand? Immediately.

(She hangs up. She digs out a cigarette and lights it and paces.)

Oh, my God, she's …
She does this. She just goes off.
But she's an artist for God's sake she needs solitude and …
and with HIM, for God's sake.
But …
but she's taken her pills with her.

Of course she could be leaving him.
She could be coming here.
There's really no need to … Oh, God!

(She rushes back to phone, picks it up and presses a button.)

Sir James.
I'm sorry.
No, there's something of a mix-up going on in Paris.
I don't know if you have children but …

Well then you know how …
how helpless and desperate one feels for their well-being
when one is thousands of miles away.

No, no, it's just my daughter Pegeen.
You've probably met her, Pegeen Vail, the artist?
Are you sure?
Surely you've heard of her?
No, Pegeen.
No, Pegeen.
P-E-G-E-E-N.
I'm really quite surprised you haven't.
She's extraordinary.
The state museum in Finland gave her a show and …
and one reason I was interested in your museum was because
as director of the Tate
I thought you'd be … be …
I'm sorry.
Would you mind very much if I called you back.
I'm so … I'm just so …

(She hangs up, grabs up her purse, digging in it for cigarettes as she paces. She throws purse away from her, lights up a cigarette and paces. She goes to the phone, then starts away from it, kicks her purse, as the phone buzzes. She rushes to it and immediately presses the button.)

YES, YES? *(Pause.)* Who?
The prefecture of …
Put him through.
For Christ's sake, Pegeen, for …

Oui!
Bonjour, monsieur le prefecture.
Oui. Je suis Peggy Guggenheim.
Yes … my daughter.
Ma petite fille.

(She stares forward. Suddenly she cries out. behind her the light through the Venetian bars brightens to scarlet. Blackout.)

End of Part Three

PART FOUR

In the gondola on the water. Sounds of water are heard over Peggy who is speaking in the dark.

PEGGY.

Piano. Piano, Guido. Lentemente.
Every night … at sunset.
we go like this.
Guido and I.

(Sparkling blue-green light comes up on Peggy. She lies stretched out on her side downstage center. She is in a gondola. Suspended directly above her is a horizontal full-length mirror. Both Peggy and the reflection of her full form seem suspended in mid-air. Sound of water and of someone leisurely rowing fill the air. The light is all blue and green and shadow. Pause.)

Si, si. Piano, Guido, piano.
On the Canallazzo … at sunset.
The *capalavero.*
My favorite time of day.
Seeing the sun … watching the sun sink …
into the dark, deep, down … sea.

I've settled my children … my collection.
The lawyers … they settled it today.
They'll stay here, my children.
Right here.
In their home.

Not the Louvre. It was sweet revenge to say no to them.
Not the Tate nor the Metropolitan nor any of the National Galleries of Art.

I've signed it all over …
do you believe it?
To my ugly uncle's museum in New York.
Family after all!

But it'll be here.
Intact in my home.
They've promised.
But even better … the lawyers have it …
in writing.
So we will always remain here in this city that floats on water.
And always in this light. This magnificent light of Venice.

Lentemente, Guido.
As if making love.

He did, my Guido, make love to me once.
Here in this gondola.

It was wonderful.
He's asked again, but …
I told him it had never happened.
"C' è un sogno," I told him.
"Solamente un sogno."

He reminded me … too much …
of my old soldier boy.
My … hero of the Somme …
who loved my nose.

Look. Look. All these beautiful palazzos … lined up along the canal like women … beautiful women … haunted by beauty … contemplating the reflections before them … in a glass.
Sinking, fading, floating.
All floating … the houses, cafes and *campos*
in time marked only by tides.

Lente, Guido …
let's drift … drift … drift … to sea.

I saw him …

saw Guido … when she was here …
watching my Pegeen.

He didn't see me watching.

How bright his eyes were …
when he looked on my Pegeen.
Slim.
Blond …
delicate goddess.

Too fragile …
to be mine.

Look!
There!
See it?
The moon.

Reflected in water she's
Pollack!
His mad moon woman!
Fragmented in horizontals of infinite tactile value.

Nothing's there.
Nothing but light.
Shimmering … jagged light …
A moon goddess …
reflected in …
refracted in …
my own …
my very
own …
eyes.

(Sounds of water continue. Lights fade out.)

End of Play

PROPERTY LIST

Dresses, shoes, purse, jewelry
Sheaf of papers
Cigarettes, lighter
Sunglasses, reading glasses
Towel
Glass, bottle of gin
Tissues
Bottles of nail polish
Ashtray
Wastebasket
Aerosol can

SOUND EFFECTS

Running water
Knocking
Phone ringing
Phone buzzer
Water

NEW PLAYS

★ **THE EXONERATED by Jessica Blank and Erik Jensen.** Six interwoven stories paint a picture of an American criminal justice system gone horribly wrong and six brave souls who persevered to survive it. "The #1 play of the year…intense and deeply affecting…" *–NY Times*. "Riveting. Simple, honest storytelling that demands reflection." *–A.P.* "Artful and moving…pays tribute to the resilience of human hearts and minds." *–Variety*. "Stark…riveting…cunningly orchestrated." *–The New Yorker*. "Hard-hitting, powerful, and socially relevant." *–Hollywood Reporter*. [7M, 3W] ISBN: 0-8222-1946-8

★ **STRING FEVER by Jacquelyn Reingold.** Lily juggles the big issues: turning forty, artificial insemination and the elusive scientific Theory of Everything in this Off-Broadway comedy hit. "Applies the elusive rules of string theory to the conundrums of one woman's love life. Think *Sex and the City* meets *Copenhagen*." *–NY Times*. "A funny offbeat and touching look at relationships…an appealing romantic comedy populated by oddball characters." *–NY Daily News*. "Where kooky, zany, and madcap meet…whimsically winsome." *–NY Magazine*. "STRING FEVER will have audience members happily stringing along." *–TheaterMania.com*. "Reingold's language is surprising, inventive, and unique." *–nytheatre.com*. "…[a] whimsical comic voice." *–Time Out*. [3M, 3W (doubling)] ISBN: 0-8222-1952-2

★ **DEBBIE DOES DALLAS adapted by Erica Schmidt, composed by Andrew Sherman, conceived by Susan L. Schwartz.** A modern morality tale told as a comic musical of tragic proportions as the classic film is brought to the stage. "A scream! A saucy, tongue-in-cheek romp." *–The New Yorker*. "Hilarious! DEBBIE manages to have it all: beauty, brains and a great sense of humor!" *–Time Out*. "Shamelessly silly, shrewdly self-aware and proud of being naughty. Great fun!" *–NY Times*. "Racy and raucous, a lighthearted, fast-paced thoroughly engaging and hilarious send-up." *–NY Daily News*. [3M, 5W] ISBN: 0-8222-1955-7

★ **THE MYSTERY PLAYS by Roberto Aguirre-Sacasa.** Two interrelated one acts, loosely based on the tradition of the medieval mystery plays. "… stylish, spine-tingling…Mr. Aguirre-Sacasa uses standard tricks of horror stories, borrowing liberally from masters like Kafka, Lovecraft, Hitchock…But his mastery of the genre is his own…irresistible." *–NY Times*. "Undaunted by the special-effects limitations of theatre, playwright and *Marvel* comic-book writer Roberto Aguirre-Sacasa maps out some creepy twilight zones in THE MYSTERY PLAYS, an engaging, related pair of one acts…The theatre may rarely deliver shocks equivalent to, say, *Dawn of the Dead*, but Aguirre-Sacasa's work is fine compensation." *–Time Out*. [4M, 2W] ISBN: 0-8222-2038-5

★ **THE JOURNALS OF MIHAIL SEBASTIAN by David Auburn.** This epic one-man play spans eight tumultuous years and opens a uniquely personal window on the Romanian Holocaust and the Second World War. "Powerful." *–NY Times*. "[THE JOURNALS OF MIHAIL SEBASTIAN] allows us to glimpse the idiosyncratic effects of that awful history on one intelligent, pragmatic, recognizably real man…" *–NY Newsday*. [3M, 5W] ISBN: 0-8222-2006-7

★ **LIVING OUT by Lisa Loomer.** The story of the complicated relationship between a Salvadoran nanny and the Anglo lawyer she works for. "A stellar new play. Searingly funny." *–The New Yorker*. "Both generous and merciless, equally enjoyable and disturbing." *–NY Newsday*. "A bitingly funny new comedy. The plight of working mothers is explored from two pointedly contrasting perspectives in this sympathetic, sensitive new play." *–Variety*. [2M, 6W] ISBN: 0-8222-1994-8

NEW PLAYS

★ **MATCH by Stephen Belber.** Mike and Lisa Davis interview a dancer and choreographer about his life, but it is soon evident that their agenda will either ruin or inspire them—and definitely change their lives forever. "Prolific laughs and ear-to-ear smiles." *–NY Magazine.* "Uproariously funny, deeply moving, enthralling theater. Stephen Belber's MATCH has great beauty and tenderness, and abounds in wit." *–NY Daily News.* "Three and a half out of four stars." *–USA Today.* "A theatrical steeplechase that leads straight from outrageous bitchery to unadorned, heartfelt emotion." *–Wall Street Journal.* [2M, 1W] ISBN: 0-8222-2020-2

★ **HANK WILLIAMS: LOST HIGHWAY by Randal Myler and Mark Harelik.** The story of the beloved and volatile country-music legend Hank Williams, featuring twenty-five of his most unforgettable songs. "[LOST HIGHWAY has] the exhilarating feeling of Williams on stage in a particular place on a particular night…serves up classic country with the edges raw and the energy hot…By the end of the play, you've traveled on a profound emotional journey: LOST HIGHWAY transports its audience and communicates the inspiring message of the beauty and richness of Williams' songs…forceful, clear-eyed, moving, impressive." *–Rolling Stone.* "…honors a very particular musical talent with care and energy…smart, sweet, poignant." *–NY Times.* [7M, 3W] ISBN: 0-8222-1985-9

★ **THE STORY by Tracey Scott Wilson.** An ambitious black newspaper reporter goes against her editor to investigate a murder and finds the *best* story…but at what cost? "A singular new voice…deeply emotional, deeply intellectual, and deeply musical…" *–The New Yorker.* "…a conscientious and absorbing new drama…" *–NY Times.* "…a riveting, tough-minded drama about race, reporting and the truth…" *–A.P.* "… a stylish, attention-holding script that ends on a chilling note that will leave viewers with much to talk about." *–Curtain Up.* [2M, 7W (doubling, flexible casting)] ISBN: 0-8222-1998-0

★ **OUR LADY OF 121st STREET by Stephen Adly Guirgis.** The body of Sister Rose, beloved Harlem nun, has been stolen, reuniting a group of life-challenged childhood friends who square off as they wait for her return. "A scorching and dark new comedy…Mr. Guirgis has one of the finest imaginations for dialogue to come along in years." *–NY Times.* "Stephen Guirgis may be the best playwright in America under forty." *–NY Magazine.* [8M, 4W] ISBN: 0-8222-1965-4

★ **HOLLYWOOD ARMS by Carrie Hamilton and Carol Burnett.** The coming-of-age story of a dreamer who manages to escape her bleak life and follow her romantic ambitions to stardom. Based on Carol Burnett's bestselling autobiography, *One More Time.* "…pure theatre and pure entertainment…" *–Talkin' Broadway.* "…a warm, fuzzy evening of theatre." *–BrodwayBeat.com.* "…chuckles and smiles of recognition or surprise flow naturally…a remarkable slice of life." *–TheatreScene.net.* [5M, 5W, 1 girl] ISBN: 0-8222-1959-X

★ **INVENTING VAN GOGH by Steven Dietz.** A haunting and hallucinatory drama about the making of art, the obsession to create and the fine line that separates truth from myth. "Like a van Gogh painting, Dietz's story is a gorgeous example of excess—one that remakes reality with broad, well-chosen brush strokes. At evening's end, we're left with the author's resounding opinions on art and artifice, and provoked by his constant query into which is greater: van Gogh's art or his violent myth." *–Phoenix New Times.* "Dietz's writing is never simple. It is always brilliant. Shaded, compressed, direct, lucid—he frames his subject with a remarkable understanding of painting as a physical experience." *–Tucson Citizen.* [4M, 1W] ISBN: 0-8222-1954-9

DRAMATISTS PLAY SERVICE, INC.
440 Park Avenue South, New York, NY 10016 212-683-8960 Fax 212-213-1539
postmaster@dramatists.com www.dramatists.com

NEW PLAYS

★ **INTIMATE APPAREL by Lynn Nottage.** The moving and lyrical story of a turn-of-the-century black seamstress whose gifted hands and sewing machine are the tools she uses to fashion her dreams from the whole cloth of her life's experiences. "...Nottage's play has a delicacy and eloquence that seem absolutely right for the time she is depicting..." *–NY Daily News.* "...thoughtful, affecting...The play offers poignant commentary on an era when the cut and color of one's dress—and of course, skin—determined whom one could and could not marry, sleep with, even talk to in public." *–Variety.* [2M, 4W] ISBN: 0-8222-2009-1

★ **BROOKLYN BOY by Donald Margulies.** A witty and insightful look at what happens to a writer when his novel hits the bestseller list. "The characters are beautifully drawn, the dialogue sparkles..." *–nytheatre.com.* "Few playwrights have the mastery to smartly investigate so much through a laugh-out-loud comedy that combines the vintage subject matter of successful writer-returning-to-ethnic-roots with the familiar mid-life crisis." *–Show Business Weekly.* [4M, 3W] ISBN: 0-8222-2074-1

★ **CROWNS by Regina Taylor.** Hats become a springboard for an exploration of black history and identity in this celebratory musical play. "Taylor pulls off a Hat Trick: She scores thrice, turning CROWNS into an artful amalgamation of oral history, fashion show, and musical theater..." *–TheatreMania.com.* "...wholly theatrical...Ms. Taylor has created a show that seems to arise out of spontaneous combustion, as if a bevy of department-store customers simultaneously decided to stage a revival meeting in the changing room." *–NY Times.* [1M, 6W (2 musicians)] ISBN: 0-8222-1963-8

★ **EXITS AND ENTRANCES by Athol Fugard.** The story of a relationship between a young playwright on the threshold of his career and an aging actor who has reached the end of his. "[Fugard] can say more with a single line than most playwrights convey in an entire script...Paraphrasing the title, it's safe to say this drama, making its memorable entrance into our consciousness, is unlikely to exit as long as a theater exists for exceptional work." *–Variety.* "A thought-provoking, elegant and engrossing new play..." *–Hollywood Reporter.* [2M] ISBN: 0-8222-2041-5

★ **BUG by Tracy Letts.** A thriller featuring a pair of star-crossed lovers in an Oklahoma City motel facing a bug invasion, paranoia, conspiracy theories and twisted psychological motives. "...obscenely exciting...top-flight craftsmanship. Buckle up and brace yourself..." *–NY Times.* "...[a] thoroughly outrageous and thoroughly entertaining play...the possibility of enemies, real and imagined, to squash has never been more theatrical." *–A.P.* [3M, 2W] ISBN: 0-8222-2016-4

★ **THOM PAIN (BASED ON NOTHING) by Will Eno.** An ordinary man muses on childhood, yearning, disappointment and loss, as he draws the audience into his last-ditch plea for empathy and enlightenment. "It's one of those treasured nights in the theater—treasured nights anywhere, for that matter—that can leave you both breathless with exhilaration and...in a puddle of tears." *–NY Times.* "Eno's words...are familiar, but proffered in a way that is constantly contradictory to our expectations. Beckett is certainly among his literary ancestors." *–nytheatre.com.* [1M] ISBN: 0-8222-2076-8

★ **THE LONG CHRISTMAS RIDE HOME by Paula Vogel.** Past, present and future collide on a snowy Christmas Eve for a troubled family of five. "...[a] lovely and hauntingly original family drama...a work that breathes so much life into the theater." *–Time Out.* "...[a] delicate visual feast..." *–NY Times.* "...brutal and lovely...the overall effect is magical." *–NY Newsday.* [3M, 3W] ISBN: 0-8222-2003-2